THE WORLD

OF THE

OLD TESTAMENT

A CURIOUS KID'S GUIDE TO THE BIBLE'S MOST ANCIENT STORIES

BY MARC OLSON
ILLUSTRATED BY JEMIMA MAYBANK

beaming books

MINNEAPOLIS

Text copyright © 2019 Marc Olson
Illustration copyright © 2019 Beaming Books

Published in 2019 by Beaming Books, an imprint of 1517 Media. All rights reserved.
No part of this book may be reproduced without the written permission of the publisher.
Email copyright@1517.media. Printed in Canada.

25 24 23 22 21 20 19   1 2 3 4 5 6 7 8

ISBN: 978-1-5064-5059-9

Library of Congress Control Number: 2019946135

Beaming Books
510 Marquette Avenue
Minneapolis, MN 55402
Beamingbooks.com

TABLE OF CONTENTS

INTRODUCTION

This is a book about the Bible. Sort of. It's about discovering more about the Bible by exploring the ancient world in which the Bible's stories were born and grew up.

According to the Bible story, the Hebrew people migrated and moved through the lands of Mesopotamia, Egypt, and Canaan during the thousand or so years between the time Sarah and Abraham received a promise from God and the days when a nation of wilderness-weary folks came to reside in the lands along the river Jordan. For the next thousand years, the people settled into this promised place, trying their best to honor and obey the God who made them a nation.

This book is about that time and those lands and the amazing people and things and mysteries that existed there and then. Using the tools of scholarship, archaeology, sociology, and history, it presents insights and facts about the people, locations, and events of the ancient places where the Bible was born. We call it a guide with the hope that it will help time travelers like you see the sights and understand a little bit about the locals as you explore their world.

Where Are We?

This book focuses on a big boomerang-shaped swath of green on the map that bends around the dry Syrian desert. In the East it touches the Persian Gulf. In the North it swoops beneath the mountains of what today we call Turkey. In the West it scoots along the Mediterranean Sea and stretches south along the great Nile River. Some call it the Fertile Crescent because of this bend shape. Some call it the Cradle of Civilization because it's where some of the greatest inventions in human history had their start. For more than 10,000 years, all kinds of human beings, in hundreds of languages, have called it home.

- The Bible locates the Garden of Eden between the Tigris and Euphrates—two rivers that still exist today.

- The city of Ur is held to be the hometown of Abraham and Sarah. The distance between here and Canaan, where Abraham and Sarah ended up, is 10,000 miles.

- The Mediterranean is the earth's largest sea (based on surface area). The name *Mediterranean* means "middle of the earth." ★

- The Sinai Peninsula has a landmass of 23,000 square miles, about the size of Lake Huron.

When Are We?

The earliest stories in the Bible are set more than 5,000 years ago. Scholars tell us Sarah and Abraham most likely left the city of Ur around 1800 BCE—almost 2,000 years before the birth of Jesus.

2500 BCE

Between 7 BCE and 6 CE

Jesus is born.

In putting this book together, we went looking for information. And here's the thing about ancient information: there's not a lot of it. So this book consists of the following:

WHAT WE KNOW

There are some documented facts about the ancient world. These come from written sources or other artifacts that have survived over the years, including the Hebrew Bible.

WHAT WE THINK WE KNOW

Based on these ancient witnesses, we make some assumptions and projections that seem to make sense. We have very likely made mistakes.

WHAT WE KNOW WE DON'T KNOW

An awful lot.

WHAT WE DON'T KNOW WE DON'T KNOW

Our vision of the ancient world will always be incomplete—especially as we try to look further and further back in time. But we can study and imagine the people who lived and the places that existed even 4,000 years ago, trusting that they'll tell us something about our own time.

But be warned.

This book may very well change the way you read, understand, experience, and even feel about the Bible and the stories it contains. Just as a magnifying glass can transform a backyard or strip of city woods into a strange and fascinating new world, so also the windows and lenses and looks offered here can help you see the old, old Bible in some new and exciting ways.

- At 4,132 miles, the Nile River is the longest in the world. It flows north.
- Mt. Sinai (AKA Mt. Horeb) is about 7,500 feet tall. That's half the height of Mt. Whitney, the highest peak in the continental United States, and about a quarter the height of Mt. Everest.
- Jericho is possibly the oldest continuously inhabited city in the world, with evidence of habitation as early as 10,000 BCE.
- People have lived in Jerusalem for more than 6,000 years.

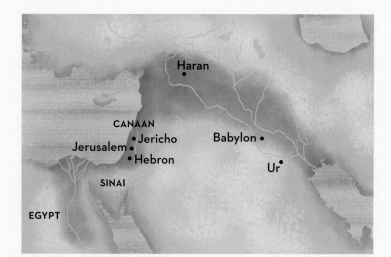

476 CE	1163	1215	1601	1861	1969
Rome falls.	The Notre Dame Cathedral is built.	The Magna Carta is written.	Shakespeare writes *Hamlet*.	The US Civil War starts.	Neil Armstrong walks on the moon.

MYTH AND HISTORY

Myth and history are two different ways of telling stories. **History** tries to tell stories that create an accurate record. **Myth**, meanwhile, doesn't necessarily mean "something that didn't happen." It's more about telling a story that offers a meaning or explanation within the experience of life. Both types of storytelling were widely used in ancient Mesopotamia—and both are used in the Bible!

Ancient people mixed myth and history

The difference between these two kinds of storytelling isn't always clear. In the Bible, mythic stories are told about historic events and people, and historical stories include mythic events and elements. It's not always clear what kind of story is being told. The difference between history and myth in Bible stories is a question that has preoccupied people for centuries.

TWO TYPES OF STORYTELLING

	Myth	History
Method	Myths use compelling stories, situations, and characters. Sometimes these characters were regular people.	History tracks big moments of special interest, and usually concerns itself with powerful people like military leaders, priests, and kings.
Purpose	Explain, educate, entertain, and explore. Myths take on big questions like "Why do people do bad things?" or "Why doesn't everyone in the world speak the same language?"	Make sure that people, events, and outcomes get remembered. Sometimes, history was used by the powerful to make sure things got remembered in a certain way—one that made them look good!
Means of communication	Myths often got started as stories told around campfires, passed from generation to generation for centuries—before they were finally written down later.	History was recorded in writing, with monuments, and in pictographs or stone carvings.

📖 IN THE BIBLE

- Many of the stories in the first chapters of Genesis contain mythic elements. These stories answer questions about why things are the way they are. For instance, the story of the Fall (Gen. 3) offers answers for everything from why childbirth hurts, why work is hard, to why humans tend to find snakes creepy!

- The story of Noah and the flood contains an explanation of where rainbows come from!

- The story of the tower of Babel gives an explanation for why people don't all speak the same language.

- The lists of kings of Israel and Judah in 1 and 2 Kings and 1 and 2 Chronicles read a lot more like history than myth.

MESOPOTAMIA 3000 BCE

Mesopotamia means "between two rivers." It's an ancient name for the even more ancient floodplain between the Tigris and Euphrates rivers. Mesopotamia is called the Cradle of Civilization because all kinds of important things were discovered, invented, and born here.

📖 MESOPOTAMIAN MUD IN THE BIBLE

- The land between the rivers is the setting for the creation story—and the Garden of Eden (Genesis 2:14).

- God made the first human being from good Mesopotamian clay (Genesis 2:6-7).

- The Plain of Sumer is called "Shinar" in Genesis. It's where the Tower of Babel was built—out of mud bricks (Genesis 11:1-4).

Clay nail

Pillow-shaped bricks

Wooden handle

Beating hammer

Baked clay

The Sumerians were among the first inhabitants of this region. They lived in the southern third of the land from about 5000 BCE until 1750 BCE. Their civilization was made up of city-states. Some of the first ones were Uruk, Nippur, and Ur.

The Sumerians were responsible for inventing advanced agriculture, soap, sailboats, cities, schools, writing, and the wheel.

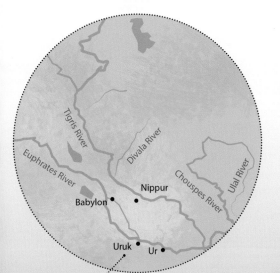

The city of Uruk is thought to have been the oldest city in the world.

The Sumerians built their cities on artificial mounds to protect them from floods.

Attracted by all the food and other wealth in the cities, various mountain tribes occasionally invaded. Often they stayed and became part of city life.

Mesopotamian cities' walls and buildings were made of mud bricks, which were mixed with straw and baked in the hot sun. These bricks were hard as stone—until a hard rain came and they would melt!

The great rivers of the plain watered the crops that fed the cities. The rivers also moved trade goods—and sometimes flooded with little warning.

The artisans of Mesopotamia were masters of mud! They used their local clay to make sickles, axes, hammers—and even nails.

AGRICULTURE 3000 BCE

The Plains of Sumer

The ancient Sumerians had to change their environment to make it a good place to live. By building embankments and levees to tame and direct the rivers, draining the too-wet areas, and digging out canals to move water where they needed it, the Sumerian farmers were able to produce enough barley and other grains to feed thousands of people—and support whole cities.

The sun was hot and rain was scarce, so the river was essential.

Simple levees and dikes were made of piled-up earth. They needed to be repaired constantly.

All the labor was done by hand—including digging miles of irrigation canals.

📖 IN THE BIBLE ·

- For his disobedience, Adam was cursed with the hard labor of farming (Genesis 3:17-19).

- Cain is described as the first farmer and the founder of a city (Genesis 4).

Not Just Here

While the early civilizations of Mesopotamia get the credit for inventing this kind of big-scale farming, advanced agriculture started at about the same time along Egypt's Nile River, and in the Indus River Valley of India. The rivers, and their regular floods, made it all possible.

Ancient crops included barley, emmer (a kind of wheat), chickpeas, lentils, bitter vetch, onions, olives, melons, grapes, sesame, and flax. Sumerians also harvested sugary dates from the date palms that grew in the delta.

The rivers also provided fish—and ways to move stuff by boat.

Sumerian government and religion were both built around planning and managing the huge amounts of hard labor and trade that made their settled city life possible. Laws and taxes and writing were invented to manage water and land rights and keep track of everything.

Ancient Mesopotamian creation stories say that the gods decided to make human beings because they were tired of having to do hard work. According to these myths, humans were created to dig irrigation canals.

- When Lot chose where to settle, he looked for well-watered farmland (Genesis 13:10-11).

- Joseph was in charge of storing and distribution of grain for all of Egypt (Genesis 41:46-57).

NOMADS

Cities grew up beside the great rivers of Egypt and Mesopotamia, where growing crops and storing grain made it possible for large groups of people to settle down in one place. But some tribes and clans thrived by moving around. We call them nomads.

Nomads were herders instead of farmers. Traveling in groups of extended family, they followed their flocks of cattle, goats, sheep, and (later) camels, moving season by season in search of water and green grass for the animals. Nomads survived by breeding and raising these animals for their wool, milk, and meat.

What their animals and the wilderness didn't provide, nomads traded for, making deals with farmers and artisans in the cities and towns they visited.

📖 IN THE BIBLE

- The story of Cain and Abel describes an age-old tension between city dwellers and nomadic herders. Abel was a herder, while Cain was a farmer. Cain's envy about God's favor for Abel led to the first murder (Genesis 4:1-8).

- Abraham and his family were nomadic herders (Genesis 13:2-7).

- Abraham and Sarah's descendants—the children of Israel—herded animals and lived in tents for generations until they migrated to Egypt (Genesis 47:1-6).

- The first dwelling place made for God was a traveling tent made from goat hair (Exodus 26:7). According to 2 Samuel 7:6-8, God was just fine with this arrangement.

Nomads lived in tents made from felted goat hair or sheep's wool spread over a frame made of wooden poles. The tents were portable, remained cool and shady in the heat of the day, and held warmth during cold nights. The inside area of these large tents could be divided by curtains into separate sections for hospitality, men's quarters, and space for women and children. Sometimes very young, sick, or injured animals were brought inside.

Some ancient Mesopotamian literature gets pretty snobby about the herding people, calling them slobs and vagabonds, and accusing them of wearing dirty animal hides and eating raw meat. City people were often suspicious of nomads, who would show up unexpectedly and upset the social order that made urban life work.

HOUSE

In the ancient world, *house* meant much more than a structure where people lived. The word was used to describe the extended family, all one's possessions—or a city, a tribe, or even an entire nation. All of these things were referred to as "houses."

The Israelites built houses with three or four rooms around a central courtyard or garden. This design allowed for privacy from the street while including fresh air and space for small livestock inside. Rooms were square or rectangular, and approximately 10 by 12 feet. The rooftops were accessible by ladders, and were places to cook, as well as to sleep and stay cool at night.

Very wealthy people, and kings, showed their power and importance by building with logs of cedar imported from the Phoenicians, and with carefully cut stone. These luxuries were far beyond the means of most people. The wealthy could also afford more space, with wider homes and bigger rooms, including servants' quarters and storerooms.

Among the cultures of Canaan, ancient housemates also sometimes included dead ancestors. When a beloved family member died, sometimes their bones would be buried in the floor beneath the household shrine. Daily incense and food rituals that honored the household gods also included veneration and appreciation of the ancestors.

Houses were inhabited by families, which usually included all the unmarried children of the household, as well as any servants or slaves. In most societies of the ancient Near East, married sons continued to live in the houses of their fathers, bringing their wives and children into the growing household. This often meant adding rooms and even more stories to city houses, or building new structures beside the old in rural areas.

Hammurabi of Babylon (1792–1750 BCE) is responsible for writing what is probably the first building laws in history. The Code of Hammurabi contained 282 laws; number 229 reads: *"If a builder builds a house for someone, and does not construct it properly, and the house which he built falls in and kills its owner, then that builder shall be put to death."* The Hebrew Bible also includes laws about building safety.

📖 IN THE BIBLE

- Pharaoh described his kingdom as a house, and set Joseph in control of it (Genesis 41:38-43).

- Israel's twelve tribes were descended from their ancestral houses (Exodus 6:14-19).

- God sent frogs to invade the domestic spaces of the Egyptians, including their ovens and mixing bowls (Exodus 8:1-3).

- The Hebrews' experience of captivity in Egypt is described as being "in the house of slavery" (Deuteronomy 8:14).

- Rahab's house was built into the wall of Jericho. In addition to a rooftop work area, she had a window that opened to the outside of the city's wall (Joshua 2:6-15).

- An ancient building code calls for safety on the rooftop (Deuteronomy 22:8).

- The temple at Shiloh was called the house of the Lord (1 Samuel 1:7).

- The Philistine god's temple was called his house (1 Samuel 5:2).

- Hiram of Tyre sent wood and workers from the wealth of Phoenicia to make David a fine house (2 Samuel 5:11).

- As David promised to build a temple, God plays with the meanings of the word house (2 Samuel 7:1-29).

NAMES

In the ancient world, names held more meaning than you could fit neatly on a nametag. A person's name not only identified who they were, but also communicated all kinds of beliefs, ideas, and information. A good name carried with it power and luck. A bad one might stick you with curses.

Gods

Some names linked the named person to a deity.

Sin-nada was a common Sumerian name for either a man or a woman. It means "the moon god is praised." In Akkadian, the royal name *Nebuchadnezzar* means "Nabu protect my eldest son." Nabu was the name of an Assyrian and Babylonian god of wisdom, letters, and writing.

It's possible that newborns in Egypt weren't named until they survived the most dangerous weeks and months of early childhood. Babies who died without being named were called "Osiris" for the Egyptian underworld god.

The Israelites used names to honor their God too. The names *Elijah*, *Jeremiah*, and *Isaiah* all include part of the name *Yahweh*. *Israel*, *Daniel*, and *Ezekiel* use the more general name "El" for God.

• •

Parents didn't always name their children after gods. *Secular* names simply communicated the way the baby came into the world, or described something remarkable or unique about them.

In the Bible, twin brothers Jacob ("he takes by the heel") and Esau ("hairy") were named for the way their birth happened and what the older brother looked like when he was born..

• •

Dramatic life events sometimes brought a name change. Changing a name was one way to demonstrate that the new person was different from the old in a deep and meaningful way. In the Bible, perhaps the most famous name change happened when Abram and Sarai became Abraham and Sarah.

Babylonian women who married sometimes took names that honored their husbands ("My Husband Is My Happiness" or "She Found the King of Her Heart"). Priests and priestesses often took names that emphasized their religious devotion. Members of the court also sometimes changed their names to show loyalty to the king or the nation ("The Country Is Glad" and "The King Is My God").

IN THE BIBLE

• God gave new names to Abram and Sarai as part of the covenant promise that they would become parents of a great nation (Genesis 17:1-22).

....

• Jacob got a new name (Israel) after he survived a heavenly wrestling match (Genesis 32:28).

....

• Benjamin was named "Son of My Sorrow" by his mother Rachel, who died shortly thereafter. His name was later changed by his father (Genesis 35:18).

....

• Joseph's Egyptian wife was called Asenath—Egyptian for "devoted to the goddess Neith" (Genesis 41:50).

....

• *Moses* is an Egyptian name (Genesis 2:10).

....

• God promised to save the people from shame and defeat and give them a new name (Isaiah 62:2).

FOOD

In the ancient world, where you lived was the most important factor in what you ate. Without refrigeration, easy ways to transport food, or grocery stores, people ate what they could grow or raise on the land where they lived. Cooks and bakers worked with what they had.

Barley was the most important grain in Mesopotamia. A type of wheat called emmer was plentiful in Egypt. By 2600 BCE bakeries in Egypt had invented pancakes and produced about fifty different types of bread—including sourdough.

Where the farmland was fertile, people ate pretty well. As always, the wealthy ate better than the poor. The rich liked rich and exotic food. Hunters in Egypt sometimes went after hippos!

Sheep, goats, and cows produced milk, which people turned into cheese, yogurt, and a kind of curdled cross between buttermilk and cottage cheese. These animals, as well as pigs and ducks, were also butchered for meat.

Wine and beer were a huge part of Mesopotamian and Egyptian life. The wealthy drank wine. Everybody drank beer.

Fruits that grew in the region included dates, figs, grapes, olives, melons, and pomegranates. The Sumerians also enjoyed pistachio nuts.

Storing grain allowed towns and cities to keep food to be used in years when the crops weren't as plentiful. Extra grain also meant trade with others.

Onions and garlic and leeks seasoned lentil and bean stews.

HONEY

Bread and onions were the common people's staples.

EGYPT

If not for the amazing Nile River, Egypt wouldn't have been much to look at. But because of that mighty river snaking through the desert, Egypt was one of the most stable, successful, and powerful nations in the ancient world. It still exists today.

Aside from its tremendous wealth, ancient Egypt was known for its grand building projects—like the pyramids of Giza, which were built by 2500 BCE.

The Nile's annual flooding was so reliable and regular that the Egyptians built their calendar around it. The gentle floods deposited a yearly load of deep, dark silt that fertilized the crops and allowed Egypt's farmers to plant up to three crops a year.

PHARAOH

Egypt was one of the first nations to have one king, called the pharaoh, rule over a large region that included many cities. Rule passed down through the royal family in what's called a dynasty. The pharaoh had the power of life and death, and owned all of the land. Everybody who lived in Egypt was a servant, guest, or slave to Pharaoh. When he was wise and kind and benevolent, this worked great. If he was selfish or cruel, things tended to fall apart.

📖 IN THE BIBLE

- The Bible references Egypt more than 600 times. Egypt is portrayed as a place of refuge, help, wealth, success, and particularly oppression in the book of Exodus, when God's people were enslaved there for hundreds of years.
- Abraham went to Egypt during a time of famine (Genesis 12:10).
- Joseph gets sold to a caravan of traders bringing exotic incense and spices into Egypt (Genesis 37:25-28).
- God announces to Moses that he will rescue the people from their captivity in Egypt (Exodus 3:7-10).
- In order to make a powerful alliance, King Solomon gets married to the daughter of a pharaoh (1 Kings 3:1).

Egypt's river and crops gave Egyptians tremendous wealth that they used for trade. On the river and via caravan routes through the desert, they traded their food, pottery, gold, and linen textiles for all the things they couldn't grow or find at home.

And what crops! In addition to papyrus that made paper and flax which they spun and wove into fine linen fabric, Egyptians enjoyed plenty of fruit and grains and vegetables.

GODS

• •

Egypt's wealth led ancient Egyptians to celebrate their gods' generosity and power. The greatest Egyptian gods included Amun-Ra, the king of the gods who was associated with the sun; Tarwat, the goddess who protected women in childbirth; and Osiris, the god of the afterlife.

SLAVERY

In the ancient world, everything was made by hand, and all work was done by people. Whether it was farming, raising children, tending flocks of sheep or goats, digging canals, or building pyramids, human hands, backs, and bodies did it. As villages grew into cities and the need for large-scale agriculture grew, people started looking for sources of cheap or free labor, and the institution of slavery was invented.

People in debt could sell themselves into slavery to pay what they owed. The head of a household could also sell a child or other relative. Often this was for a specific amount of time or type of work. We know about these arrangements through written contracts that detailed how they worked, and how the buyers and sellers agreed on price and duration, and sometimes how the slave was allowed to be treated.

Some slaves were cared for as members of the family—but others were treated no better than animals.

📖 IN THE BIBLE

- Abraham and Sarah owned slaves. The ones we know by name include Hagar and Eliezer (Genesis 15:1-3; 16:1).
- Years of famine in Egypt eventually caused almost everybody to sell themselves as slaves to Pharaoh (Genesis 47:20-21).
- The Hebrews' experience of slavery in Egypt was a huge deal for the way they thought of themselves and their laws about making, owning, and freeing slaves (Deuteronomy 15:12-15; Leviticus 25:39-46).
- King Solomon made slaves of neighboring nations, but refused to enslave his own people (1 Kings 9:15-22).

The first slaves were often captured prisoners of war. When one city or nation conquered another, the winner would take a bunch of people from the loser and put them to work at home. The Sumerian word for "slave" was "foreign person."

In Egypt, in Canaan, and among the Israelites, too, slaves came from captured foreigners as well as nearby neighbors. Some slaves became the property of a city or its temple. Other slaves belonged to the king.

WOMEN

The cultures of the ancient Near East were patriarchal, which means men had the highest status in the household and the clan. But in several cultures, women had rights and powers that were equal or nearly equal to those of men.

In ancient Egypt, for instance, the law recognized women's and men's rights as the same. Egyptian women could choose whom to marry, or whether to marry at all. They could also sign legal contracts, adopt children, own and sell property, and be an executor for a will. A widowed or divorced woman was able to keep and run her home without needing any man's permission. Egypt even had a female pharaoh: Hatshepsut, who ruled for nearly twenty years (1479–1458 BCE).

Even when they enjoyed more rights, women were expected to keep the household functioning, raise young children, and make sure everybody was fed and clothed.

Scholars estimate that the job of grinding grain to make flour would have taken at least two hours of a woman's time every day. And once the flour was ground, she still had to make dough and bake the bread.

Childbirth was dangerous for both women and babies. Midwives helped mothers through labor, delivery, and the early weeks of infant care.

In Mesopotamia and Egypt, women were the first professional beer brewers. Sumerian alewives ran taverns in which patrons drank through long straws. Women also brewed beer at home as part of the family meal.

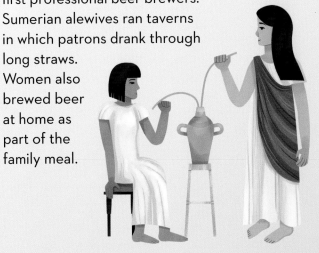

Some religions had female deities who were models for female power, authority, and independence. Women served as priestesses, "wise women," and religious leaders in the temples of Egypt and Mesopotamia.

Women were skilled weavers. In most cultures it was women who turned raw materials like wool, flax, and cotton into thread, yarn, and fabric.

The world's first author whose name we know was a Mesopotamian priestess named Enheduanna. Her poetry, hymns, and reflections are still read and studied today.

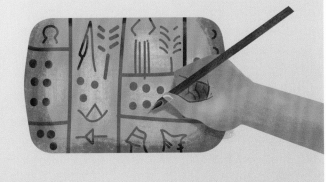

📖 IN THE BIBLE

- The Old Testament reflects the patriarchal society in which the stories were set, and in which the Bible was compiled. Ninety percent of the people named in the Bible are men. But the Bible does contain the stories of many intelligent, brave, and resourceful women who are an important part of the story of God's people.
- Sarah's Egyptian slave, Hagar, is the only person in the whole Bible who gives God a new name because of what God did for her (Genesis 16:13-16).
- Hebrew midwives sabotaged Pharaoh's plan to kill Hebrew babies (Exod. 1:15-22).
- Grinding grain is identified as women's (and slave's) work (Exodus 11:5; Isaiah 47:2; Job 31:10; and Ecclesiastes 12:3).
- Deborah is named as a prophetess and also a judge (Judges 4:4).
- An ideal wife is depicted as a smart and industrious housekeeper (Proverbs 31).
- Women's skill at spinning is recognized by Moses (Exodus 35:25-26).

THE CHARIOT 1450 BCE

The most powerful and feared weapon of war for more than a thousand years was the two-wheeled, horse-drawn chariot. Its speed, maneuverability, and ability to terrify foot soldiers made the chariot the weapon of choice—for those who could afford them. Powers such as Egypt and Assyria added chariot corps to their armies, and expanded their empires in every direction. Chariots were also prizes when captured in battle. Ancient war records include the number of chariots won from enemies.

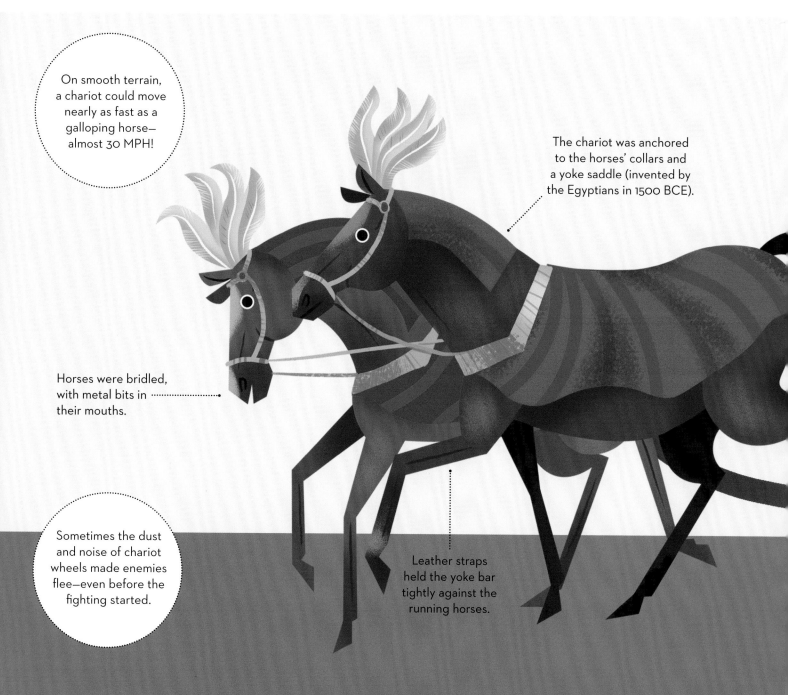

On smooth terrain, a chariot could move nearly as fast as a galloping horse—almost 30 MPH!

The chariot was anchored to the horses' collars and a yoke saddle (invented by the Egyptians in 1500 BCE).

Horses were bridled, with metal bits in their mouths.

Sometimes the dust and noise of chariot wheels made enemies flee—even before the fighting started.

Leather straps held the yoke bar tightly against the running horses.

📖 IN THE BIBLE

- Joseph arrived in his (Egyptian!) chariot to reunite with his father, who thought he was dead (Genesis 46:29).

- Sometimes, the enemies proved to be too strong, even with God's help (Judges 1:19).

This chariot is the Egyptian style of battle chariot, used around 1450 BCE. Horses, chariots, and the composite bow were introduced to Egypt only a few hundred years earlier, by a Semitic tribe called the Hyskos who came to live in Egypt around 1700 BCE. The Egyptians didn't invent the chariot, but many think they came close to perfecting it.

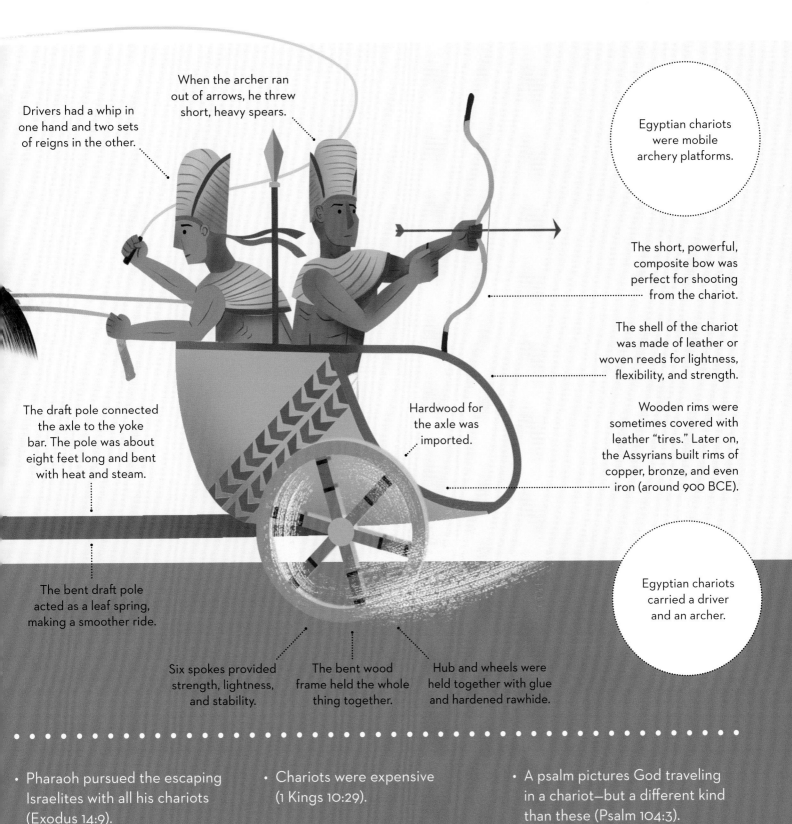

Drivers had a whip in one hand and two sets of reigns in the other.

When the archer ran out of arrows, he threw short, heavy spears.

Egyptian chariots were mobile archery platforms.

The short, powerful, composite bow was perfect for shooting from the chariot.

The shell of the chariot was made of leather or woven reeds for lightness, flexibility, and strength.

The draft pole connected the axle to the yoke bar. The pole was about eight feet long and bent with heat and steam.

Hardwood for the axle was imported.

Wooden rims were sometimes covered with leather "tires." Later on, the Assyrians built rims of copper, bronze, and even iron (around 900 BCE).

The bent draft pole acted as a leaf spring, making a smoother ride.

Egyptian chariots carried a driver and an archer.

Six spokes provided strength, lightness, and stability.

The bent wood frame held the whole thing together.

Hub and wheels were held together with glue and hardened rawhide.

- Pharaoh pursued the escaping Israelites with all his chariots (Exodus 14:9).

- Chariots were expensive (1 Kings 10:29).

- A psalm pictures God traveling in a chariot—but a different kind than these (Psalm 104:3).

IDOLS

Each city in the ancient Near East had a temple for a patron god or goddess. The people believed that this deity protected and defended them. Ancient people knew their idols weren't literally gods—but they believed that their gods would live in idols to bless and guard the people. If the statues were defiled or disrespected, the gods might depart, leaving the people unprotected.

In the center of these temples priests took care of special statues in shrine rooms far from public view. The statues were thought to contain the actual presence and power of the god or goddess they represented. They were called idols or images by others, but the people whose religion included these objects simply called them gods.

Idols were made using valuable materials, such as aromatic wood and precious metals like gold and silver. They were often painted to look lifelike, wore clothing and jewelry, and held symbolic objects. Bigger than a human being, they stood or sat in royal poses. Every day, priests would set fresh food and drink and incense in front of the gods, and the statues would be bathed, be anointed with oil, and have their clothes washed and changed.

One of the most important yearly festivals in Egypt was the Opet festival, honoring the god Amun with a huge procession. It was super popular. The people were treated to free bread and beer, and the celebrating went on for nearly a month.

📖 IN THE BIBLE ●

- Unique among ancient Near Eastern gods, God refused images and statues. One of the most persistent messages in the Old Testament is against idols (Exodus 20:3-4).

- The Israelites were to avoid eating food that had been sacrificed to idols (Exodus 34:15).

- Kissing idols is a big problem (1 Kings 19:18; Hosea 13:2).

- God could make even the idols of Egypt tremble (Isaiah 19:1).

- God's prophets made fun of idols, calling them "scarecrows" (Jeremiah 10:5).

At home, people worshiped and took care of more personal and approachable family gods. These minor deities were believed to watch over the household.

Idols weren't always stuck in their temples. During festivals the statues would be carried into the streets of the city on portable shrines. The people would go nuts for this—singing songs or chanting praise to the deity.

- Near the end of his life, Solomon, supposedly Israel's wisest king, started to worship other gods (1 Kings 11:5-8).

- Like in the temples of Egypt and Babylon, the central shrine in the Jerusalem temple was a priests-only place where God was

- Made from fine wood and gold, the Ark of the Covenant was believed to hold God's presence and power (1 Samuel

DIVINATION

For as long as humans have had any kind of religion, people have tried to make contact with the gods. Seeking inside information from the spirit world is the primary purpose of the ancient magic called divination. In the ancient Near East, divination was practiced in every culture, using all kinds of methods. Diviners practiced skills and techniques that could be taught and learned, and divination was treated like a science.

People sought the help of diviners for all kinds of questions about the present and the future, and to help find lost objects or people. Diviners helped military commanders consider strategies and consulted with farmers about when to plant or harvest. They were hired by kings to answer all kinds of questions, from whether or not to build a temple or other monument to when the time was right for something like getting married or going hunting.

Astrology was another method of divination: the belief that the position of stars and planets could affect events on earth. Astrologists throughout the ancient world used their observation of the heavenly bodies to make predictions. They kept careful records and charts of the stars' and planets' positions and movements.

- **Egyptians** watched the stars as a way to interpret and understand the timing of events.
- **The Babylonians** didn't see heavenly events as the causes of events on earth, but more like warnings—possible signs of things that were about to happen.
- **Mesopotamian** astrologers believed the gods showed themselves in their corresponding planets or stars. Bad omens attached to a particular planet showed that the god was disturbed or angry, and the king or priests could try to appease the god through sacrifice.

One way diviners got information from the spirit world was by looking for omens in the natural world. Omens occurred naturally in things like weather, celestial events, abnormal births, strange animal behavior, earthquakes, and eclipses. Diviners looked for anything out of the ordinary. Everything could have meaning or importance, from the movements of the stars to the way smoke from incense floated in a room.

The most widespread and common of these practices, though, was extispicy—the art of looking for marks or patterns in the bloody entrails of sacrificed animals. The diviner would look at the liver, lungs, colon, and heart. The shape, color, and position of these organs were used to predict the weather, gauge the loyalty of allies or the strength of enemies, and comment on the luck or fortune of activities like going to war or digging a canal.

📖 IN THE BIBLE

- Joseph is described as an interpreter of dreams (Genesis 37:5-9) and a diviner (Genesis 44:4-6).
- The Bible is most often against divination (Leviticus 19:26).
- Instead of using these practices, God's mode of communication with the people would be through prophets (Deuteronomy 18:9-20).
- Before he was king, David consulted lots to discern what he ought to do (1 Samuel 23:9-12).
- When neither dreams nor the sacred lots nor the words of prophets worked for him anymore, Saul employed a medium to raise the ghost of the prophet Samuel. Samuel wasn't pleased (1 Samuel 28:3-18).
- The prophets Isaiah (47:13) and Jeremiah (10:1-2) both condemned astrology.
- The prophet Ezekiel described the Babylonian king as using no fewer than four types of divination—including liver consultation—as he prepared to attack Jerusalem (Ezekiel 21:21-22).
- Zechariah mocked mediums and worried about how they misled the people (Zechariah 10:2).

A practice called augury looked for omens in the patterns of birds in flight. This method was used to determine whether or not the gods favored the proposed course of action.

Some diviners used special techniques rather than waiting for omens to appear. These methods included rolling dice and casting lots (kleromancy), shooting arrows (belomancy), watching flames (pyromancy), and looking in mirrors (enoptromancy).

- Some diviners, called mediums, accessed information from the spirit world by calling on the spirits of the dead or communicating with other spiritual beings and forces like household gods and demons. Mediums were believed to be able to serve as channels through which the ghost or god could speak or share knowledge.
- Ancient mediums used rituals that could include skulls and other talismans from the person whose spirit they sought to contact.
- Some mediums spent the night in sacred or holy places in order to receive a dream from the gods or spirits associated with the place.
- Egyptian spirit mediums, known as rehket, used magic to summon spirits of the dead to answer questions. They could also send them to haunt an enemy's dreams!

CANAAN

Ancient sailors in the Mediterranean Sea looked at the western shore of this land and called it the Levant—the land of the rising sun. Today, it contains Israel, Palestine, Jordan, and parts of Lebanon and Syria. From ancient times, it has been known as Canaan.

People have lived in Canaan from as early as 10,000 BCE, inhabiting the coastal plains, the cool highlands, and the oases of the Jordan River valley. They built walled cities like Jericho, Shechem, Gezer, and Jerusalem. Their tribes and clans were never unified as an ethnic or political nation, like their Egyptian neighbors to the south or the Israelites who came to power in the area around 1000 BCE, but the people did share enough similar language and cultural traditions for outsiders to refer to them all as "Canaanites" and their place in the world as Canaan.

The name *Canaan* may mean "reddish purple"—a reference to the scarlet and purple dyes produced in the area. It could also mean "brought low" or "humbled"—referring to the fact that the Canaanites were often on the losing end in fights with their more powerful neighbors.

This strip of land was the easiest overland route between Egypt and the kingdoms of Mesopotamia to the East and the Hittite realm to the north. As they passed through, exploring, trading, or waging war, these cultures intermingled their religion, arts, and technology with Canaanite society and culture.

📖 IN THE BIBLE

- "Canaan," a son of Ham, was one of Noah's grandsons, and the ancestor of the tribes who came to inhabit the land called Canaan (Genesis 10:15-20).

- God promised the land of Canaan to Abraham's descendants (Genesis 15:18-21).

- As the Israelites prepared to enter and settle in the land of Canaan, God identified the attractiveness of the local gods as a problem (Exodus 23:23-32).

- Over the course of about a hundred years, Israel's first three kings, Saul, David, and Solomon, established an Israelite kingdom in Canaan that stretched from the Sinai wilderness all the way to the Euphrates River (1 Kings 4:21 & 24).

Without big rivers like the Nile, Tigris, or Euphrates, the Canaanites relied on rainfall to water their wheat crops, orchards, and vineyards. They worshiped fertility gods, including Ba'al, who owned all the fertile land and was responsible for storms. His symbol was the bull.

Although they built city-based temples like their neighbors, Canaanites also worshiped their gods outside, building sacrificial altars of piled-up stones on mountains and hills, called "high places."

JERICHO A CANAANITE CITY

Human beings have lived beside the oasis of Jericho for more than 10,000 years. It's one of the oldest continuously inhabited places in human history. It has been called The City of Palms, City of the Moon, and The Place of Fragrance. We don't know what they called it as early as 8,000 BCE, but Jericho had enough people living in it then to build one of the first walled towns in the world—including a tower that stood more than 20 feet tall.

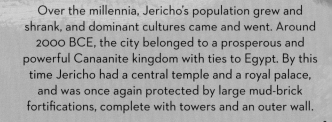

Over the millennia, Jericho's population grew and shrank, and dominant cultures came and went. Around 2000 BCE, the city belonged to a prosperous and powerful Canaanite kingdom with ties to Egypt. By this time Jericho had a central temple and a royal palace, and was once again protected by large mud-brick fortifications, complete with towers and an outer wall.

As with all real estate, location matters most. Jericho sits near the southern end of the Jordan River valley beside a reliable spring of fresh water, and along the best travel route in the whole region. Whoever controlled Jericho also controlled the fords across the Jordan. Traders moving between the ancient and wealthy lands of Egypt, Mesopotamia, and Anatolia came through Jericho all the time, bringing news, inventions, religions, culture, and amazing stuff along with them.

By 1700 BCE, Jericho's connection to Egypt was deep, especially among the upper classes, who adopted Egyptian fashions, including makeup and jewelry. The Egyptian name for the city was Ruha. Apparently, this relationship soured; it's likely that the great walls of Jericho were broken down, and the city sacked and burned, by an angry pharaoh around 1550 BCE. It would take another couple hundred years to rebuild the city, but Jericho's geographic importance and natural resources meant that people would always figure out how to live there.

📖 IN THE BIBLE ·

- Joshua led the Israelite army in an attack on Jericho's famous walls (Joshua 6).

- The prophet Elisha gets credit for performing a miracle by which God made the water of Jericho's spring sweet (2 Kings 2:15-22).

- Israel's enemies captured the strategically important city of Jericho and held it for years (Judges 3:12-14).

WEAPONS

The farmer-fighters of ancient Sumer used pretty much the same tools for warfare as they did for hunting. They had shields, probably made from wood and leather. As weapons, they carried clubs, knives, bows, spears, and slings. The Sumerians also invented a chariot of sorts; theirs had four solid plank wheels and was drawn by oxen.

Composite bow

Invented by Asiatic nomads before 2000 BCE, the composite bow, made from horn, wood, and sinew, could shoot farther than previous bows, and with enough force to pierce leather armor. By 1500 BCE, chariot armies all over the Fertile Crescent were using composite bows to decimate their opponents.

Bundle bow

This primitive bow was made of sticks bundled together and tied with string. It would be replaced by much more effective bows-and-arrows in later centuries.

Bronze Age—3000 BCE

Bronze sickle sword

Invented in Sumer by around 2500 BCE, this sword was probably modified from a grain-harvesting sickle.

Sumerian Soldier—2500 BCE

The armies of Canaan and Israel fought each other with infantries armed with swords and spears made of copper or bronze. They wore leather armor fitted with copper metal scales. These soldiers were backed up by groups of archers and slingers, who rained baseball-sized stones against their enemies.

Horses and chariots

The two-wheeled chariot changed warfare. Armies that could afford horses and chariots had the advantage of speed and power, and could quickly overtake soldiers on foot. In chariot battles, opposing forces flew straight at each other in pass after pass, shooting arrows the whole time. Once one of the sides was slowed enough, armed and armored fighters would run in and throw spears or hack away with swords.

Iron Age—1000 BCE

The most significant change in ancient weaponry happened when people figured out how to smelt iron from iron ore, using high heat from charcoal fires.

Iron weapons

Iron was stronger than any other metal used at the time. Because iron ore was much more common than the copper and tin that make bronze, iron weapons could be made almost everywhere. The Hittites were the first to smelt iron on a wide scale, by around 1500 BCE, and they had a military advantage because of it for almost 200 years.

Iron armor and boots

Assyrian Soldier—600 BCE

The soldiers of Assyria used all the technological advances in weaponry to become the most fearsome warriors the region had ever seen. Assyria used its military might to build a huge empire, and the Assyrians show up in many of the stories of the Old Testament as fearsome enemies of the Israelites.

IN THE BIBLE

- The Philistine giant, Goliath, is described as having bronze weapons and armor (1 Kings 17:4-7).

- Philistine inhabitants of the coastal plain weren't easily conquered because of their iron weapons (Judges 1:19).

- David had warriors who could fight with either hand (1 Chronicles 12:1-2).

WAR

Six thousand years ago, warfare hadn't really been invented. Violence was common, and every town had its share of fighters, but there was no such thing as an organized army. But as cities grew into kingdoms and nations, kings and other leaders decided that fighting was not only necessary for defense, but also a good way to gain power, amass wealth, and build influence (as long as you won).

In the beginning, soldiers were part-time farmers. Fighting was done in the season between the planting and harvest times. Because everybody had to grow food in order to eat, warfare took second place to the work of farming. It didn't take long for these town militias to become standing armies, creating a whole new class of professionals and all kinds of weapons and war-fighting technologies.

📖 **IN THE BIBLE** •

- God tried to calm soldiers who might be frightened (Deuteronomy 20:1).

- God commanded the Israelites to be utterly merciless in battle (Joshua 8:1-8).

- The prophet Jeremiah described vivid battle scenes against Babylon (Jeremiah 51).

Not all fighting was done on land. With major rivers at the heart of their lands, both Egypt and the Mesopotamian kingdoms, as well as the Phoenicians of the Mediterranean coast, had skills in naval warfare. In this era, navy battles were fought at close quarters, with oar-propelled ships ramming each other while fighters shot arrows and hurled stones at their enemies.

Siege warfare
Armies were the primary tools for building empires. This involved not only defending the home kingdom, or fighting on open ground, but also attacking and conquering enemy cities—which were often on hills, fortified with high walls, and filled with angry people with lots of weapons. The Neo-Assyrians of 900–600 BCE were the best at conquering cities. The Assyrian army had engineers who built earth and rock ramps, wheeled towers that could deposit soldiers atop city walls, and battering rams with iron tips that blasted through bronze gates. This image portrays what a siege might have looked like.

Around 1180 BCE, Pharaoh Ramses III defended Egypt from an invasion by a group known as the Sea Peoples. Rock slingers and archers on the decks of the Egyptian boats helped push the enemy ships close enough to the shoreline for land-based fighters to overwhelm them. Navy battles were fierce and deadly, and not as common as land wars.

- The Israelite army had rules for besieging enemy towns (Deuteronomy 20:19-20).

- The Babylonian king, Nebuchadnezzar, lay siege to Jerusalem (2 Kings 25:1-11).

- The prophet Isaiah offers a vision of the world without war (Isaiah 2:1-4).

COVENANT

In the ancient world, the most important deals and agreements weren't treated as regular business transactions. Whether they were made between dear friends, families making a marriage pact, or rival kingdoms negotiating a peace treaty, the most powerful agreements created a whole new relationship. They included promises as well as threats, blessings, divine witnesses, and usually a dead animal or two. They were called covenants.

Sometimes, both parties to the agreement walked between the cut-up parts of a sacrificed animal, as if to say, "Let this happen to me if I don't do as I promised." After the sacrifice, the two parties could eat the animal together as a sign of friendship and trust.

Official Witnesses included gods, as well as all kinds of natural forces: mountains, rivers, heaven and earth, wind, storms, and clouds. Breakers of the covenant weren't just rebelling against human beings, but against the highest powers around.

A **Bloody Ritual** sealed the deal. Because the stakes in a covenant were usually life-or-death, someone shed some blood to make the agreement solemn and binding. Sometimes one or both parties cut themselves and shed blood to show how committed they were.

Naming the Players. The more powerful partner in the agreement was identified as the giver of the covenant. This included all the titles of the giver (Venerable One, Lord of Two Lands, Revered One, The Shepherd, etc). If the parties had equal standing, they both got named.

A **Prologue** told a history of the relationship, emphasizing the past generosity of the covenant giver, playing up the benefits of good relationship, and suggesting that keeping the covenant was a show of thanks.

Obligations described the specific payment or action that would benefit the more powerful partner. Covenants also usually included a requirement that the weaker party couldn't enter into covenants with anybody else.

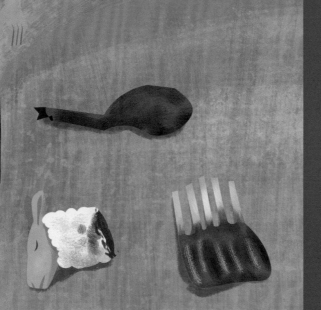

Curses and Blessings spelled out the results of both disobedience and obedience. Curses for disobedience included disease, famine, exile, and total destruction. Blessings could be anything from peace, long life, and prosperity, to sunshine and rainbows.

Sometimes each party would drink a little bit of the other's blood—this is where the idea of "blood brothers" comes from.

IN THE BIBLE

- As described in the Bible, the God of the Hebrews was unique among ancient deities. Instead of just witnessing or enforcing commitments between people or nations, God takes part in covenants—including their obligations!

- God made a covenant with Noah that bound God to a promise (Genesis 9:8-17).

- God's long-term covenant with Abraham included cutting up animals (Genesis 15:7-18) and cutting people, too! (Genesis 17:7-14).

- Abraham made a covenant with Abimelech (Genesis 21:27-32).

- God made probably the most important covenant with the Hebrew people, with clouds and thunder and fire as witnesses (Exodus 19:3—20:18).

- David and Jonathan made a covenant of friendship and love (1 Samuel 18:1-4).

POWERS

The ancient Near East consisted of many small tribes and kingdoms that were constantly at war with each other for power and influence. But sometimes, a single kingdom or city-state grew to be a major power, building an empire that covered most of the region. These empires brought scattered cities and regions under the control of a single ruler, but this unity came at a heavy price—the great powers often ruled with terrible violence, exiled or enslaved the peoples they conquered, and demanded tribute from the kingdoms under their control.

The Big Powers

The Hittites

The Hittites were a major force in the north of the region from 1600 to 1200 BCE. Their empire was known as the Kingdom of Hatti. The Hittites regularly battled Egypt up and down the Mediterranean coast, and were one of the first peoples to make iron tools and weapons.

The Assyrians

At the height of its power, around 650 BCE, the Assyrian Empire controlled nearly the entire region—including much of Egypt. The Assyrians maintained their empire with remarkable cruelty, using violence and torture to keep conquered peoples afraid, and exiling tribes across the known world so that even the cultures of the lands they conquered would be lost or forgotten.

The Egyptians

Egypt exercised enormous influence throughout the region, reaching the height of its power around 1100 BCE.

The Phoenicians

Famous as sailors, builders, fine artisans, and traders, the Phoenicians had access to in-demand cedar trees for timber, are responsible for the phonetic alphabet, and were famous for the purple dye they produced.

The United Kingdom of Israel

According to the Bible, the lands of the twelve tribes of Israel were united into a single kingdom by its most famous ruler, David. David and his son Solomon expanded their influence by capturing strategic border towns in neighboring kingdoms, but their empire wasn't on the same level as those of powers like Assyria or Egypt. The single Israelite kingdom lasted for less than eighty years (1000-922 BCE) before revolt divided the nation into the kingdoms of Israel in the north and Judah in the south.

Philistines

The Philistines were known as fierce fighters. Perpetual opponents of the tribes of Israel, they occupied the coastal cities of Ashkelon, Ashdod, and Gaza as early as 1200 BCE.

Aram Damascus

Centered in their capital city of Damascus, Aram Damascus (sometimes referred to as "Arameans" in the Bible) had small independent kingdoms across parts of the region.

The Northern Kingdom

The kingdom of Israel was more prosperous, possessing fertile valleys and several port cities—but all that wealth attracted the attention of the Assyrian Empire. King Shalmaneser V conquered Israel in 722 BCE and scattered most of the population to cities and towns across Mesopotamia.

The Southern Kingdom

Judah managed to avoid conquest by Assyria for years, but its capital, Jerusalem, with its central shrine to the Lord, was finally captured and destroyed by the Babylonians in 586 BCE.

Ammon

The Ammonites were shepherds and herders, and had access to limestone and sandstone for building and trade.

Moab

The kingdom of Moab lay along a major trade route between Syria and the Red Sea, called "The King's Highway." The Moabites were known as sheep breeders. Moab was conquered by the Babylonians in 582 BCE.

Edom

Edom had access to copper, and was a source of mining and smelting for itself and its neighbors. The Edomite kingdom fell to the Babylonians around the same time as Moab.

Israel and Its Neighbors (950 BCE)

KINGS

Kings didn't appear right away in human culture—rather, they emerged as ancient cultures grew and changed.

In the tribes and towns of early Mesopotamia, the leaders were the people most familiar with the needs and desires of the gods. Holy people like shamans, priests, and priestesses supervised planting and harvest rituals, and kept the community in line by pleasing and praying to the deities. This worked fine for a long time.

As cities got a little bigger and started to trade and fight with one another, the ancients saw the need for leaders who could combine the god-connected role of the priests with some military muscle and a little flash. The Sumerians called their first kings *lugal*—which means "big man."

As time went on, size and strength alone weren't enough to make a perfect king. In every part of the ancient Near East, kings came to embody all the best qualities of leadership and humanity: smarts, wisdom, humility, power, decisiveness, religious piety, charm—even physical beauty and musical skill. In some countries, like Egypt, kings were seen not just as leaders appointed by the gods, but as actual gods on Earth.

The Israelites' Most Celebrated King
Young
Handsome
Brave
Musical!

Distinctive headgear

Big ears and eyes mean he's perceptive and wise.

Groomed beard and mustache and fancy clothes show status.

Exaggerated muscles and size show he's a strong leader.

The sword is an emblem of power.

Wide, confident stance

📖 IN THE BIBLE

- God warned the people about what happens when a nation gets a king (1 Samuel 8:14-22).

- Saul's size and strength made him a perfect *lugal* (1 Samuel 10:23-25).

- David was chosen as king—even though he was not a typical candidate (1 Samuel 16:6-8).

- Solomon had the ideal combination of kingly qualities (1 Kings 4:20-34; 1 Kings 10:23-25).

- David was the royal recipient of God's blessing and authority (2 Samuel 7:8-9).

As a nomadic people, the descendants of Abraham and Sarah existed as a collection of tribes for almost a thousand years before deciding they needed a king. During those years, leadership fell to patriarchs like Abraham and Jacob, prophets such as Moses and Samuel, and judges like Deborah and Gideon. For the children of Israel, God granted authority to lead for specific situations and moments.

WEALTH

The first wealth was food. Nations like Egypt that were lucky enough to have access to reliable water, good farmland, and lots of labor could raise more food than they needed to survive—then trade that food to become very wealthy.

Kings displayed their wealth and boasted about their riches as a way of showing how powerful they were and warning other kings not to mess with them. The kings of Mesopotamia displayed their wealth by building huge cities and stone statues of themselves, and especially by erecting lavish temples for their gods and palaces for themselves. These palaces were furnished with exotic and amazing objects from all over the world. Some palaces even included zoos, featuring plants and animals from every corner of the known world.

War was another way of becoming wealthy. Powerful empires conquered neighboring kingdoms, stole all their wealth and valuables, then made the conquered nations—called vassals—pay them a yearly tribute of goods, gold, and slaves. This kept the riches pouring in to the winning nation.

Gold wasn't a very useful metal—it was soft, and could bend and break easily. But as soon as wealthy kings started to notice gold's shine and its resistance to tarnishing, the metal became desirable as a way for the rich to show off their wealth. Gold became known as the metal of the gods, and was used to decorate and furnish temples and palaces, as well as to adorn the necks, ears, noses, wrists, arms, and ankles of the wealthy in every culture.

Gold and silver measured wealth by weight, and became a convenient means to collect taxes and tributes. Names for weights, like *mina*, *shekel*, *talent*, and *deben*, later became the names of coins.

Because of its proximity to the Nile, Egypt was among the richest nations in the ancient world. Egyptian cities developed amazing arts and crafts that were in demand all over the known world, and traded these goods for copper, lead, precious stones, oil, herbs, gold, and other goods from other countries.

Probably the most well-known of Egypt's pharaohs, Tutankhamun reigned during the New Kingdom period, from about 1332 to 1323 BCE. His tomb was discovered in 1922, and its contents, including more than 5,000 objects, show a little of the enormity of Egypt's wealth and the importance of the king. Tutankhamun's funeral mask was made with 22 pounds of gold.

📖 IN THE BIBLE

- Abraham's servant described his master's wealth (Genesis 24:34-35).
- A famine in Egypt showed how quickly grain became more important than money (Genesis 47:13-19).
- Knowing how attractive gold and silver were, God outlawed idols made from these metals (Exodus 20:23).
- Solomon spent seven years building a monumental temple for God, and thirteen years building his own house—almost twice as big. Both used the best and most expensive materials and construction (1 Kings 6:1—7:12).
- Solomon's wealth is described in terms of horses and chariots (2 Chronicles 1:14-17).
- On his way toward building an empire, King David defeated his enemies and took their wealth, extracting tribute payments from Moab and the Arameans of Damascus (2 Samuel 8:2-7).
- Egypt imposed a new king in Jerusalem and required a tribute payment (2 Chonicles 36:1-4).
- Ezekiel describes God's chariot as the showiest and most amazing imaginable (Ezekiel 1:4-28).
- The book of Esther begins with a description of the Persian king's wealth (Esther 1:1-7).

CLOTHES

Clothing in human civilization began as a way to stay alive—to protect the body from cold and the elements. But humans usually want more than simple survival. People in every climate soon invented more efficient, beautiful, and comfortable ways of clothing themselves. And once the basics got figured out, it turned out that clothes could be a way to demonstrate wealth or status or rank.

The Egyptians were into comfort and beauty, and their climate was warm. Their fabric was linen, made from flax, which was native to the Nile valley. Woven linen has been part of Egyptian culture since 5000 BCE. Linen fabric is light and breathable, and the Egyptians loved it.

Linen can be woven so finely that it's nearly see-through. The ancient Egyptians, who liked showing off their bodies, enjoyed this.

In the beginning, clothing was very simple. That is to say, human beings started wearing clothes so they could stop being naked all the time. The first clothes didn't look like boxer shorts, though. They were likely a variation on the blanket; whatever worked to keep a body warm. These clothes were probably made of animal skins.

Egyptian women wore a simple sheath dress of woven linen, called a *kalasiris*. Most men—including Pharaoh himself—wore a close-fitting kilt, or skirt, called a *schenti*. Up until they adopted the short, shirt-like, tunic from nearby Syria around 1500 BCE, Egyptian men generally cruised around naked to the waist.

📖 IN THE BIBLE

- The prophet Isaiah told his people that God would defeat their enemies—even crushing their city walls (Isaiah 25:9-12).
- Jeremiah described the destruction of Jerusalem by the Babylonians (Jeremiah 39:8).
- Cities and towns without walls were vulnerable (Psalm 80:12-13; Ezekiel 38:10-12).
- Sent by the king of Persia to rebuild and restore Jerusalem, Nehemiah toured the broken walls (Nehemiah 2:13-17).
- A proverb compares a person without self-control to a broken city wall (Proverbs 25:28).

Cities in Mesopotamia were surrounded by walls made of mud bricks set on top of stone foundations. They started small, but within a thousand years, wealthy cities were making massive walls, complete with watchtowers. The wall around the city of Uruk, built by 2600 BCE, was almost five miles long and manned by up to 900 soldiers.

While mud was relatively easy to work with, stone lasted longer. Where people had access to stone and the tools to carve, or dress, it, walls—or at least foundations for walls, were built from huge stone blocks. Archaeologists recently discovered the remains of a 25-foot-high wall in the city of Jerusalem that was made in 1700 BCE from cut-stone boulders weighing as much as five tons each.

Over the centuries, the mud and clay bricks of southern Mesopotamian city walls melted back into mounds or piles—or were busted apart more quickly by enemy armies. This rubble got used as the base for rebuilt walls. Cycle after cycle of this process created artificial mounds which made the walls thicker and higher—and actually raised the elevation of the whole city!

Around 600 BCE, King Nebuchadnezzar II of Babylon had three 40-foot-high walls built around the city. They were so wide that chariots could race on top of them!

PROPHETS

Prophets were people who communicated messages from the gods. Unlike priests, who often came from noble or wealthy families and were specially trained for their roles, prophets had little or no formal training. Their work was more intuitive than that of the priests. Prophets' messages were called oracles, and they offered wisdom or news from the gods. Sometimes the oracle was positive and encouraging. Other times, it was a message of doom or judgment.

Mesopotamian prophets were called "answerers," "proclaimers," "dreamers of dreams," "ecstatics," and "crazy ones." The Israelites called their prophets "seers," "seers of visions," and "men of God." The Akkadian word for prophet means "the one who invokes god."

Most people considered prophets a little bit crazy. Prophets sometimes cut themselves, using their blood to provoke a vision. Prophets were often described as hairy and dirty and wild. They commonly fell into trances or ecstatic frenzies, after which they spoke or wrote or drew their divine message. Sometimes this looked like singing and shouting and dancing. Sometimes it looked like seizures and sickness.

IN THE BIBLE

- As someone sent with a specific message from God, Moses is seen as the first of Israel's prophets (Exodus 3:16-18).

- In a contest between prophets, the more dramatic guys lost (1 Kings 18:21-24).

- The prophet Elijah is described as a wild, hairy man (2 Kings 1:8).

- A prophet did his work and was described as a madman (2 Kings 9:1-13; Hosea 9:7).

- It was sometimes hard to tell who was a prophet and who was crazy (Jeremiah 29:26-27).

- Elisha the prophet of God used music to induce a vision (2 Kings 3:13-15).

- Isaiah describes a vision (Isaiah 6:1-8).

- Ahab consulted 400 prophets before going into battle (1 Kings 22:6).

Some prophets were directed by their respective gods to bring specific words, predictions, or messages to the king or other ruler, without being sent for. Other prophets were more like advisors—the king or ruling court could summon them with questions. Prophecy thrived during times of crisis, like warfare or famine, as people sought advice and counsel before making big decisions, or to understand why these things were happening. Sometimes, a prophet's message would explain how a problem could be fixed or resolved.

The court at Mari in modern-day Syria employed royal prophets. When consulting a group of prophets, a king would sometimes divide them into different groups to see if their messages agreed. If they did, the oracle was relied on as authentic. If they didn't, someone would be in trouble.

Speaking (or shouting, or acting weird) near the temples, in the court, or even in the marketplace or at the city gate, prophets called their people to ways of living and acting that honored and respected their god or gods. Throughout the ancient world, prophets often condemned greed, oppression, and empty religious worship. They called their people to remember and care for the poor. When it seemed like the message was resisted or rejected, they sounded warnings about divine judgment. In this way, a prophet served as a conscience for the nation.

BABYLON

Fought over, built up, torn down, loved, hated, admired, and imitated all over the ancient world, the city of Babylon was important for thousands of years. Babylon was a large port town on the Euphrates River. Legend has it that the city was established by Sargon the Great around 3000 BCE. Even from these early days, it was a center of trade, learning, and culture.

Called Esagila, the central temple, or ziggurat, was 300 feet wide on each side and rose in seven "steps" to be 300 feet tall. At the top was the blue-glazed tile temple shrine where Marduk's statue lived.

The name *Babylon* comes from the Akkadian language, and means "Gate of God."

In the year 1755 BCE, an Amorite king named Hammurabi united all of southern Mesopotamia and most of Assyria. He established Babylon as its capital. Hammurabi called the whole kingdom Babylonia. He also helped elevate the god Marduk as the patron of the city, and the chief god of the whole region.

📖 IN THE BIBLE •

- Genesis describes the founding of Babylon as an example of human pride and overreach. The authors played with the name, referring to the place as "Bavel," which means confusion (Genesis 11:1-32).

- Sitting beside the foreign river, the Jewish exiles missed their homeland and their own city (Psalm 137).

Who Ruled Babylon When

Under the reign of the Chaldean king Nebuchadnezzar II (605–561 BCE), Babylon became the largest city in the world and the center of the Neo-Babylonian Empire, whose power and influence stretched all the way to the Mediterranean Sea.

Nebuchadnezzar's Babylon is thought to have been the largest city in the world at the time, with as many as 200,000 people. The main city occupied an area of around four square miles, on either side of the Euphrates River. It boasted massive walls and fortifications, as well as a rebuilt temple and a massive gate, both covered with blue-glazed brick tiles.

Hammurabi's Babylon included walls, temples, and canals. Over the next thousand years, all this infrastructure would be destroyed and rebuilt as the city was conquered and claimed by invading armies and empires. Regardless of who ruled, however, they used the city's size and beauty to showcase their strength and smarts.

It's not difficult to understand why the people who wrote and put together the Hebrew Bible disliked Babylon so much. This was the place the Judean rulers, elites, and religious leaders were taken after Nebuchadnezzar II destroyed Jerusalem and Judah—including the Jerusalem temple—in 587 BCE.

- The prophets announced that, someday soon, Babylon would be defeated (Jeremiah 50:46; 51:58; Isaiah 13:19).

- Jeremiah described how everybody was attracted to Babylon, but how it always ended badly (Jeremiah 51:7-9).

- The Chaldean king surveyed his magnificent city (Daniel 4:28-30).

EXILE

As early as 2300 BCE, the project of empire building in Mesopotamia included capturing prisoners from rival city-states. War captives were often taken from their defeated cities and put to work as soldiers or slaves in the victor's capital or other selected spot. By the time the Assyrians were establishing an empire, starting around 1100 BCE, capturing and moving large or important groups of a defeated people's population was an established and effective part of warfare.

Deportation and resettlement were the empire's means of ensuring order in the lands they had conquered.

First to be moved were the religious and political leaders, who could start a revolt if left where they were.

It was the Assyrians who conquered the city of Samaria in Israel in 721 BCE and deported the whole population of the northern kingdom. The ten "lost tribes" of Israel weren't resettled in one place, but were dispersed all over the region, where they disappeared from history.

ASSYRIA

• Nineveh

BABYLONIA

ISRAEL

Samaria

JUDAH

Jerusalem

• Babylon

• Nippur

Next on the list were the valuable engineers and artisans and builders, whose professions and special skills would enrich or benefit the empire—but could not be allowed to rebuild the conquered nation.

Regular people and farmers were deported too. By completely scattering the conquered people all over the region, the rulers effectively eliminated the possibility of rebellion. Also, being relocated pressured everyone involved to give up their tribal identities, languages, gods, and traditions and become well-behaved members of the empire.

Between 597 and 586 BCE, King Nebuchadnezzar of Babylon deported more than 10,000 Judeans from the southern kingdom of Judah. In 586, he destroyed Jerusalem and took its king, Zedekiah, into captivity along with more than 1,000 prominent citizens, leaving a remnant of defeated and confused Judeans among the ruins of their holy city. The deported ones were settled in a town near Nippur, in Babylonia, which came to be known as Al-Yahudu, or "Judahtown."

The new community in Al-Yahudu was separate enough from surrounding Babylon that the deportees could retain their religion and identity. Though they learned to speak Aramaic, which was the language of the empire and its business, they also continued to speak Hebrew, and dedicated themselves to studying and preserving their history and sacred scripture.

 **IN THE BIBLE**

- Most surviving records of ancient deportation and warfare come from the winning side. The Bible gives a unique account of deportation from the perspective of a conquered people—including when and how some of them were allowed to return to and rebuild their homeland.

- Cain is presented as the first exile, afraid of the vulnerability of being a stranger in a strange land. God promised to protect him (Genesis 4:14).

- Jeremiah prophesied the capture and destruction of Jerusalem (Jeremiah 20:4-5).

- Nebuchadnezzar II conquered Jerusalem in 597 BCE and took the wealth, the king, and thousands of skilled workers and soldiers (2 Kings 24:10-16).

- Ten years later, the Babylonians returned to finish the job (2 Kings 25:8-12).

- The fall of the northern kingdom of Israel to the Assyrian king Shalmaneser was followed by the deportation of its people (2 Kings 17:3-6).

- The psalmist describes sadness and anger over being in exile from Jerusalem (Psalm 137).

JERUSALEM

The ancient city of Jerusalem occupies two hills, Mount Zion and Mount Moriah, in the highlands of Canaan. According to the Bible, by 1100 BCE, Jerusalem was a heavily fortified city, inhabited by a people called the Jebusites. King David captured the city in a surprise attack in 1010 BCE and made it his capital, establishing Jerusalem as the center of politics and religion.

Over its long history, Jerusalem has been destroyed at least twice, besieged more than twenty times, and captured more than forty times. It was taken by the Egyptians in 925 BCE (and again in 609 BCE) and sacked by the Philistines in 850 BCE. Jerusalem narrowly avoided conquest by the Assyrians in 701 BCE, when the Assyrian army abruptly left the battlefield.

In 587 BCE, the Babylonians, under Nebuchadnezzar II, captured Jerusalem, looted and destroyed the temple, broke down the city's walls, and deported a big part of its population—especially the elites and skilled craftspeople. This was devastating, and left the ruined city almost empty of people. When the Babylonians carried off wealthier citizens of Judah, their land was redistributed among the poor who remained. As you might expect, this later became a problem for both groups.

📖 IN THE BIBLE ••••••••••••••••••••••••••••••••••

- The first mention of Jerusalem is as the home city of a mysterious priest-king called Melchizedek, who offered Abraham bread, wine, and blessing (Genesis 14:18).

- David captured Jerusalem by sneaking up a water shaft into the city (2 Samuel 5:6-10).
- David relocated the Ark of the Covenant to Jerusalem (2 Chronicles 15:3).
- Solomon built a magnificent temple in Jerusalem (2 Chronicles 3:1).

David moved the Ark of the Covenant to Jerusalem, where it was kept in a tent. His son and heir, Solomon, built a temple to God that involved years of labor and the finest building materials available. Under David, Solomon, and later rulers such as Hezekiah, the city underwent massive construction and fortification, including the building of walls, towers, and an enormous water reservoir as well as the temple and king's palace.

After a few decades, the Persians defeated the Babylonians. The Persian king, Cyrus the Great, decreed in 539 BCE that all the Jews in Babylon could return to Jerusalem and rebuild their temple. Over the course of the next handful of years, four major groups returned to resettle the area, joining the people who had remained behind. The appointed governor, Nehemiah, led the effort to rebuild Jerusalem's walls beginning in 445 BCE.

With few years of exception, Jerusalem would go on to be ruled by foreign powers for centuries. It never again rose to the height of prosperity and power it enjoyed under its early kings. The city remained a center of worship for Jews, who refer to it as the Holy City. The city is today also a significant site for Muslims, and for Christians, who know Jerusalem as the place of Jesus' death, resurrection, and ascension.

- Jerusalem would be destroyed because of its unfaithfulness (Isaiah 29:1-3).
- Nebuchadnezzar II captured Jerusalem and destroyed it (2 Kings 25:1-10).
- King Cyrus decreed the return of the Jews to

- Nehemiah returned to rebuild Jerusalem's walls (Nehemiah 1-3).
- The holy city Zion was described as the central sign of Israel's superiority—and the center of God's kingdom on earth (Psalm 72:10).

BIOS

Marc Olson is a theologian and a former pastor. He earned a Bachelor of Fine Arts from Pacific Lutheran University, and a Master of Divinity from Luther Seminary. He was also awarded the Seminary's International Preaching Fellowship in 2007, which resulted in a year abroad, studying and teaching with his family in Tanzania, as well as in Israel and Palestine. Marc lives in St. Paul, Minnesota, with his son, Sigurd, and their Basset Hound, Bruce. He also drives a garbage truck.

Jemima Maybank is an illustrator living in Leeds, England, who is fascinated by the ancient Orthodox icons of saints found in many cathedrals of the UK. In her free time she likes running and trying to stop her houseboat from sinking.